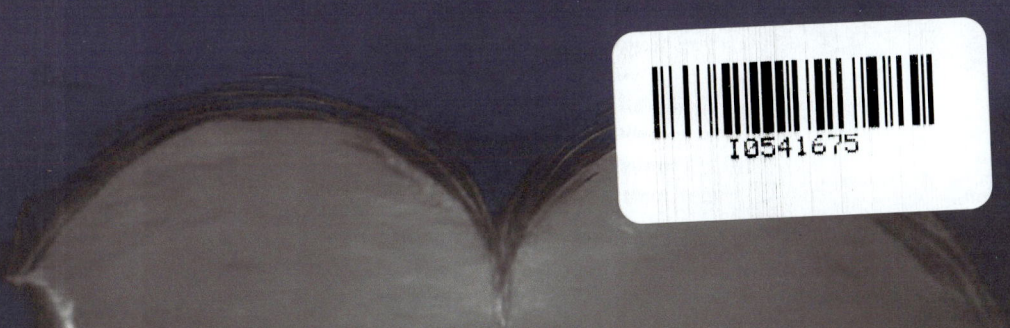

You have met your king from the King, but are you truly ready for the next step: marriage?

This Journal Belongs To:

Date:

MARRYING YOUR KING

from the

King

Barbara Nelson Bennett

New Being *Books*

Lauderhill, FL

Learn more about the author at:
https://barbaranbennett.com

Cover design by Gabyriella Foster

Edited by Annette Purkiss, Allwrite Publishing

ISBN: 979-8-9918479-2-6

Library of Congress Control Number: 2025931075

Printed in the United States of America

Author's Note

In the first part of this series, we journeyed through the sacred process of waiting on your king from the King. We explored the depth of contentment in singleness, recognizing that it is not a passive state, but a season of preparation, self-discovery, and spiritual growth. The world often tells us that singleness is a burden, but God shows us that it is a gift. Through this waiting period, we are called to refine our identity, strengthen our relationship with God, and find joy in the present, trusting that His timing is perfect.

The second book built upon this foundation, focusing on preparing yourself to be the woman God has called you to be. In that season of preparation, we examined what it means to cultivate a heart aligned with God's purpose. We delved into the importance of growing in wisdom, stewarding the gifts God has given you, and becoming the best version of yourself—not just for a future spouse, but for the glory of God. The journey to becoming a woman of strength, dignity, and grace is an ongoing process, one that requires faith, intentionality, and surrender.

Now, in this third installment, we turn our attention to what happens when God brings that long-awaited King into your life. "Marrying Your King from the King" is about understanding the beauty and sacredness of marriage from a biblical perspective. This journal is a guide for women who are stepping into or are already in the covenant of marriage, seeking to navigate this new chapter with wisdom, love, and faith.

Marriage, as God designed it, is more than just a relationship between two people—it is a reflection of Christ's love for the Church. It is both a gift and a responsibility, requiring sacrifice, grace, forgiveness, and deep spiritual intimacy. While the world often glorifies the wedding day, God calls us to look beyond that single event and focus on building a marriage that honors Him daily. This journal will guide you through understanding your role as a wife, navigating the complexities of marriage, and building a foundation rooted in God's Word.

This journey is not always easy. Marriage will test you, challenge you, and refine you, but it is also one of the most powerful avenues through which God works to sanctify you. Whether you are newly married, preparing to get married, or looking for deeper insight into your role as a godly wife, this journal will provide you with the tools and biblical truths to help you navigate the path ahead.

I was 55 years old when I got married for the first—and hopefully the last—time. I wasn't young, but God knew I wasn't ready before then. At that time, I was still a party girl, caught up in a worldly life of materialism and pleasure-seeking. I did whatever I wanted without considering God or anyone else. I was very selfish in my relationships, wanting to be catered to. I wasn't prepared to be anyone's wife in the biblical sense. If my husband had come into my life 10 years earlier, I wouldn't have been ready. I probably would have overlooked him, and he might have done the same with me.

I had to sacrifice a lot of my old self to embrace the kind of relationship I have now with my husband. My focus back then was on career and friends, but spiritually, I wasn't in the right place. That's why I created this journal—to help other women shorten their waiting time by getting ready for the man God has for them. I want women to not only recognize a man sent by God but also to develop and sustain a healthy, God-centered relationship.

In this journal, I share insights from my own marriage and dating experience for your benefit. Together, we will explore how to build a Christ-centered marriage, how to navigate challenges with grace, and how to love your spouse in a way that reflects God's love for us. Let this next chapter be one of deepening faith, growing love, and fulfilling the sacred calling of marriage. Welcome to this new journey of marrying your King from the King. Let's walk together in faith, surrendering to God's plan for your marriage, and building a life that glorifies Him.

CONTENTS

Acknowledgements, viii
Before We Begin, ix

FOUNDATIONS OF A GOD-CENTERED MARRIAGE   11
- Understanding Covenant, Not Contract
- God's Purpose for Marriage
- Preparing a Foundation That Lasts

ROLES & RESPONSIBILITIES IN MARRIAGE   23
- Understanding Submission: What It Really Means
- A Wife's Role: The Helpmeet
- Leadership and Servant-Leadership

BUILDING INTIMACY: EMOTIONAL, SPIRITUAL & PHYSICAL   35
- Spiritual Intimacy
- Emotional Intimacy
- Physical Intimacy: The Gift of Sex in Marriage

OVERCOMING CHALLENGES IN MARRIAGE   45
- Handling Conflict Biblically
- Forgiveness in Marriage
- Balancing Expectations vs. Reality

UNITY IN PURPOSE & CALLING   55
- Discovering Your Shared Purpose
- Supporting Each Other's Individual Callings
- Walking in Unity Together

BUILDING A LEGACY TOGETHER   65
- Leaving a Legacy of Faith
- Raising Children in Faith
- Building a Godly Family Foundation

PROTECTING YOUR MARRIAGE   77
- Guarding Your Heart
- Setting Healthy Boundaries in Marriage

CONCLUSION   89

AKNOWLEDGEMENTS

To my husband, Delroy Bennett—my rock. Thank you for being the man God has called you to be. You are truly my king from the King, and I am blessed to walk this journey with you.

To my sister, Audrey Nelson Campbell—thank you for always pushing me toward my greater purpose and standing by my side. Your support and encouragement mean the world to me. I couldn't ask for a better sister.

To my mother, Dorothy M. Nelson—your sacrifices and hard work have not gone unnoticed. Your labor has not been in vain, and you are deeply blessed. I love and honor you for all you've done and for the beautiful person you are.

To my son, Daner B. Hargrove—God has a plan for your life, one filled with hope, purpose, and promise. You are a blessing, a precious gift, and deeply loved. Never forget that.

To Bishop Rohan Diedrick, my mentor who baptized me and taught me how to have faith.

To Joan Quinland, my best friend and the person who witnessed to me, leading me to Christ.

To Dr. Michelle Phillips for pushing me to the limit and believing in me.

And finally to Claudine Mighty for helping me proof read this book.

BEFORE WE BEGIN...

"Marrying Your King from the King" is a journey of spiritual and practical preparation for building and sustaining a godly marriage. Each chapter is thoughtfully designed to guide you through biblical principles, personal reflections, and actionable steps to strengthen your relationship with God and your future or current spouse. Within these pages, you'll find reflective questions to deepen your understanding, prayers to center your heart on God's will, and exercises to help you apply the lessons to your own life.

This journal is divided into the following sections, each aimed at fortifying your marriage through biblical principles:

1. Foundations of a God-Centered Marriage
This section explores the principles of a covenant relationship as designed by God, emphasizing His purpose for marriage and the importance of building a foundation rooted in faith and endurance.

2. Roles & Responsibilities in Marriage
Dive into biblical insights on submission, leadership, and partnership, clarifying the roles of husband and wife while highlighting the balance between servant-leadership and mutual respect.

3. Building Intimacy: Emotional, Spiritual & Physical
Learn how to nurture spiritual, emotional, and physical intimacy as divine gifts that strengthen the marital bond and foster a deeper connection with each other and God.

4. Overcoming Challenges in Marriage
This chapter provides biblical tools for addressing conflicts, offering forgiveness, and managing expectations while maintaining harmony and growth in the relationship.

5. Unity in Purpose & Calling

Discover how to align your individual and shared callings to walk in unity, support each other's dreams, and fulfill God's greater purpose for your marriage.

6. Building a Legacy Together

Explore ways to create a lasting legacy by raising children in faith, establishing a godly family foundation, and leaving an enduring impact rooted in love and spiritual strength.

7. Guarding Your Heart & Protecting Your Marriage

Gain practical strategies for setting boundaries, safeguarding your relationship, and prioritizing your marriage to withstand challenges and honor God.

Throughout this journal, you'll find opportunities for prayer, personal reflection, and practical applications to help you on your journey. Use this time to allow God to speak to your heart, shape your spirit, and prepare your life for the incredible blessing of marriage. Trust that as you seek Him first, He will equip you to be the wife He has designed you to be with a husband specially called by Him.

Let this be your season of trusting in the King as you make plans to marry your king.

FOUNDATIONS OF A GOD-CENTERED MARRIAGE

At the heart of every marriage should be a firm foundation rooted in Christ. To have a Christ-centered marriage means that both partners are committed not only to each other but first and foremost to God. It means that Christ is the cornerstone of the relationship, guiding decisions, actions, and interactions with each other. This type of marriage is not just a partnership between two people but a union intertwined with the presence and guidance of God.

A Christ-centered marriage recognizes the spiritual significance of your union. You and your spouse are not just two individuals navigating life together, but two people called to reflect God's love through your relationship. This requires surrendering your own desires to God's will, prioritizing Him above all, and trusting Him to lead your marriage.

Ecclesiastes 4:12 "A person standing alone can be attacked and defeated, but two can stand back-to-back and conquer. Three are even better, for a triple-braided cord is not easily broken."

In a world that often equates love with emotion and romance, a Christ-centered marriage requires a deeper understanding. In a Christ-centered marriage, Christ is that third strand, strengthening and fortifying the bond between husband and wife. Without Him, the relationship is vulnerable to the pressures of life, but with Him, it becomes a force of strength, resilience, and divine purpose. The key to a lasting marriage is not merely finding someone who makes you happy but building a relationship where God is at the center. When you and your spouse rely on God to lead, your love for each other becomes a reflection of God's unchanging love for His people.

In a Christ-centered marriage, love is not merely a feeling; it is a choice. It is the decision to prioritize your partner's needs above your own, to forgive when it is difficult, to show grace when it is undeserved, and to seek reconciliation when conflict arises. This kind of love reflects Christ's love for the Church—a sacrificial love that knows no bounds. It is the kind of love that, when modeled within your marriage, serves as a beacon of hope to those around you.

Understanding Covenant, Not Contract

To fully appreciate the significance of a Christ-centered marriage, it is crucial to understand the difference between a covenant and a contract. In our society, many view marriage as a contract, a temporary agreement between two individuals based on mutual benefit. This transactional perspective creates an environment where individuals feel entitled to exit the relationship when their needs are not met. But this is not the biblical view of marriage.

A contract is rooted in self-interest, built on terms that can be modified or terminated based on circumstances. It is often riddled with conditions: "I will love you if you..." or "I will stay with you as long as you..." However, this perspective falls woefully short of the sacred commitment that God intends for marriage.

In stark contrast, a covenant is a holy promise, an unconditional commitment to one another and to God. It is a reflection of the relationship between Christ and the Church, characterized by grace, faithfulness, and mutual sacrifice. Ephesians 5:31-32 states, "For this reason a man will leave his father and mother and be united to his wife, and the two will become one flesh. This is a profound mystery, but I am talking about Christ and the church." Here, we see that marriage is designed to mirror the deep and abiding relationship between Christ and His followers. It is not merely a legal agreement but a sacred union that transcends the physical, encompassing the spiritual and emotional.

Entering into a covenant marriage means you are making a vow before God to love, cherish, and respect your spouse for life, no matter the circumstances. It is a promise to grow together, to hold each other accountable, and to seek God's will in your relationship. This commitment requires a daily, conscious choice to honor your vows, even when the love you once felt seems distant.

When conflicts arise—and they will—covenant marriage empowers you to navigate challenges with a heart set on reconciliation and healing. It fosters an environment of trust, where both partners can be vulnerable, share their fears, and seek forgiveness without the fear of abandonment. In this type of marriage, you learn to communicate openly and honestly, valuing each other's perspectives and feelings. This is the essence of living out a covenant: it reflects God's faithfulness, mercy, and love.

REFLECT

Reflect on Ecclesiastes 4:12. How can you strengthen the three-strand cord in your relationship with Christ and your partner? How can you allow God's love to flow through relationship to demonstrate a Christ-centered union?

_____

_____

_____

_____

_____

_____

_____

_____

_____

_____

_____

_____

_____

REFLECT

In what ways does viewing marriage as a covenant, rather than merely a contract, deepen your understanding of God's purpose for your relationship and the commitments you make to your spouse?

God's Purpose for Marriage

Many individuals enter marriage with the expectation that it will bring them happiness and fulfillment. While joyous companionship is indeed part of God's design, the purpose of marriage extends far beyond personal gratification. God created marriage as a means to fulfill His divine plan, which also involves spiritual growth and the advancement of His kingdom.

Genesis 2:18 "It is not good for the man to be alone. I will make a helper suitable for him."

This verse reveals God's intention for marriage: to provide companionship and partnership. It recognizes the need for human connection and the beauty of two individuals coming together to fulfill God's purposes. Your marriage is designed to enhance your personal relationship with God and to strengthen your walk with Him.

Malachi 2:15 "Has not the Lord made them one? In flesh and spirit, they are His. And why one? Because He was seeking godly offspring."

God's purpose for marriage goes beyond the couple themselves; it is also about the testimony it provides. A godly marriage cultivates an environment where children learn about relationships firsthand. It serves as a witness to others by demonstrating what it means to live out one's faith in the context of a loving, committed relationship. Moreover, marriage is a pathway for spiritual growth. In the context of a Christ-centered marriage, both partners are called to help each other grow closer to God. This involves praying together, studying Scripture, and encouraging one another in your spiritual journeys. Challenges will inevitably arise, but these can serve as opportunities for you to learn patience, forgiveness and humility. As you face difficulties, you learn to rely on each other and, most importantly, on God. Through the trials and triumphs of life, your marriage becomes a testament to God's faithfulness. It demonstrates the beauty of grace in action—the capacity to forgive, to love unconditionally, and to grow together through the highs and lows of life.

,

REFLECT

How does understanding that God's purpose for marriage extends beyond a couple, shape your perspective on your current or future relationship?

_____

_____

_____

_____

_____

_____

_____

_____

_____

_____

_____

_____

_____

REFLECT

"How does your relationship reflect God's commitment, unconditional love, and grace to those around you? In what ways can you be more intentional about demonstrating these qualities as a testimony of faith?"

_____

_____

_____

_____

_____

_____

_____

_____

_____

_____

_____

_____

_____

Preparing a Foundation That Lasts

Remember when Esther was preparing to meet King Xerxes, who ruled over the vast Persian Empire? He was not from her culture or background, yet Esther understood the importance of presenting herself in a way that honored the king's customs and expectations. She took time to prepare herself, both physically and spiritually, through self-care and adornment. This teaches us a valuable lesson about the importance of preparation and self-awareness in relationships.

Women today should embrace that same principle. Many desire marriage but haven't learned how to care for themselves fully—whether it's maintaining a polished appearance, managing their household, or growing in personal responsibility. It's not just about having a pretty face; building a strong relationship requires substance and preparation. For example, knowing how to run a home or cook can be important. I consider myself fortunate because my husband didn't mind that I couldn't cook. But I was upfront and honest about it when we were getting to know each other. Women need to be honest with men from the start. If you don't enjoy cooking or aren't skilled in the kitchen, it's better to communicate that early on rather than surprising them later. Transparency is key because it sets realistic expectations and helps build a solid foundation for the relationship."

As you navigate the complexities of marriage, remember that building a Christ-centered foundation is not a one-time event; it is an ongoing process. It requires daily commitment, humility, communication, and a willingness to seek God together. By focusing on Christ as your foundation, understanding the covenant nature of your marriage, and embracing God's purpose for your union, you equip yourselves to build a marriage that not only withstands the test of time, but also serves as a reflection of God's love to the world.

Marriage is a sacred journey—a partnership designed to glorify God and fulfill His purposes. When you allow Christ to be at the center of your relationship, you create a bond that is unbreakable, resilient, and rooted in love that transcends all understanding. This is the foundation upon which your marriage can stand strong, and this is how you honor the King by loving and serving your King.

REFLECT

How can you intentionally prepare yourself—physically, emotionally, and spiritually—for a Christ-centered relationship, just as Esther prepared to meet the king?"

_____

_____

_____

_____

_____

_____

_____

_____

_____

_____

_____

_____

_____

Fortification Prayer

Thank You for the gift of marriage and the beautiful
reflection it is of Your covenant love for us. As I prepare
my heart and life for this sacred union, help me to see
marriage not as a contract of convenience but as a
covenant of commitment—a holy bond established by
You, meant to glorify Your name and serve Your purpose.
Teach me to understand the true purpose of marriage,
that it is not simply about personal fulfillment but about
becoming a vessel of Your love, grace, and partnership in
the work of Your Kingdom. Show me how to align my
desires and expectations with Your divine design, so that
my heart is fixed on honoring You in every aspect.
Lord, I ask for wisdom and guidance as I lay the
foundation for a lasting marriage. Help me to build my
life on the rock of Your Word, cultivating a spirit of
humility, patience, and selflessness. Prepare me to be a
partner who reflects Your love, able to give and receive in
ways that strengthen the bond of unity.
Shape me into the woman You have called me to be,
equipping me with the skills, character, and faith needed
to nurture a home filled with peace, joy, and Your
awesome, loving presence.
In Jesus' name,
Amen

Work Out Your Faith:

Building Your Covenant Toolbox

Activity: Create a personalized "Covenant Toolbox" to prepare for your God-centered marriage. It is a collection of practical, spiritual, and emotional tools that align with the principles of covenant, purpose, and a lasting foundation.

Steps:
- **Reflect on Covenant**: Write down what "covenant" means to you and how it differs from a contract. Include scriptures that resonate with God's design for marriage (e.g., Ephesians 5:25-33; Genesis 2:24).
- **Clarify God's Purpose**: Create a list of your spiritual and personal goals for marriage. How will this union serve God's Kingdom and reflect His love?
- **Build Practical Skills**: Identify areas where you can grow, such as communication, conflict resolution, or managing a home. Take a small step each day toward improving each skill, such as reading a book or practicing a new habit.
- **Prayer Journal**: Dedicate a section of your journal to prayers about your future marriage, seeking God's guidance for both you and your future spouse.
- **Seek Mentorship**: Identify a godly mentor or couple whose marriage you admire and ask for their advice or support.

INSIGHT

Use this area to write additional insights from the readings, reflection questions or activity responses.

_____

_____

_____

_____

_____

_____

_____

_____

_____

_____

_____

_____

ROLES & RESPONSIBILITIES IN MARRIAGE

Understanding Submission: What It Really Means

Submission, as mentioned in **Ephesians 5:22-33,** is often a subject of discomfort and misunderstanding, particularly in today's world where independence and control are highly valued. But in the context of a Christ-centered marriage, submission is not about one person giving up their power or identity to another. It is a radical act of trust in God's design for partnership. It's about laying down our egos and pride, trusting that both spouses are equally called to honor God in their distinct yet complementary roles. Before a wife submits to her husband or a husband leads his wife, both are called to submit to Christ. This is the core of it all: mutual submission to God's authority. The moment we try to run the marriage our way—relying on our logic, our strength, or even our desires—we risk moving outside of God's purpose. There is no true submission without first surrendering fully to God, seeking His will above our own.

- **Wives Submitting to Husbands:** Submission isn't about becoming small or voiceless. It's about choosing to trust your husband's leadership while knowing that your voice still matters. It's the sacred dance of vulnerability and strength—trusting that your husband, under God's guidance, has your best interests at heart. The world might tell you that submission is weakness, but it's one of the greatest demonstrations of trust and inner strength a woman can show when she submits to a godly husband.
- **Husbands Submitting to Wives**: The command for husbands to love their wives as Christ loved the Church is not a soft, romantic suggestion. Christ's love led Him to the cross. It is sacrificial, relentless, and painful at times. Husbands are called to submit to their wives in love by laying down their lives, by sacrificing ego and selfish desires, and by leading with humility. Submission from husbands is not a passive act but a proactive, intentional effort to elevate their wives, to protect, nurture, and honor them deeply.

REFLECT

Reflect on a time when you have tried to control the outcome in your relationship. How did it impact your connection with your partner?

_____

_____

_____

_____

_____

_____

_____

_____

_____

_____

_____

_____

_____

REFLECT

When you think about the love you'll offer in marriage, do you see it as a reflection of your love for Christ, or as something you are expected to do? How can you shift your mindset to view love as a service to God?

_____

_____

_____

_____

_____

_____

_____

_____

_____

_____

_____

_____

_____

A Wife's Role: The Helpmeet

The biblical reference to being a "helper" comes from Genesis 2:18, where God says, *"It is not good for the man to be alone. I will make a helper suitable for him."* The word "helper" in this context is translated from the Hebrew word ezer, which is also used in the Bible to describe God as a helper to humanity (e.g., Psalm 121:1-2: *"My help comes from the Lord, the Maker of heaven and earth"*). The wife as a "helper," or helpmeet, can sometimes feel like a negative term in today's culture, but in the Bible, this term carries immense power. It is not a weak or passive role; it is one of great strength and divine purpose.

Being a helper, therefore, does not imply inferiority or lesser value; rather, it signifies a role of strength, support, and partnership. Just as God provides help that is essential and empowering, a wife as a helper contributes equally to the marriage in ways that complement and uplift her husband. This role underscores mutual dependence, love, and respect in a God-centered partnership.

As a wife, you are called to be a partner who brings wisdom, strength, and nurturing into the relationship. Proverbs 31 shows us a woman who is bold, industrious, and capable, yet she honors her husband and respects their unique roles in the relationship. You are a partner, not a servant. You are called to reflect the same characteristics of Christ within your marriage: strength in submission, patience in challenge, and love in all circumstances.

- **Strength and Nurture Combined:** Being a helpmeet means recognizing your unique strengths and gifts and bringing them into your marriage to build your husband up, support him in his purpose, and walk alongside him as you pursue God's vision for your lives together. Your strength isn't something to be minimized but something that complements your husband's role. It's knowing that you can be both nurturing and fierce, gentle yet immovable when necessary.

- **Empowering Your Husband:** Empowering your husband to lead isn't about stepping back but about standing alongside him. Encourage him to be the leader God has called him to be, while continuing to speak wisdom and love into his life. You are there not just to follow but to help him navigate through life's challenges as a trusted partner and friend.

REFLECT

What strengths do or would you bring to your marriage that contribute to the spiritual and emotional growth of your husband and family?

_____

_____

_____

_____

_____

_____

_____

_____

_____

_____

_____

_____

REFLECT

How can you cultivate the qualities of a godly helper by supporting, encouraging, and complementing your partner's strengths and purpose while remaining rooted in your own God-given identity?"

_____

_____

_____

_____

_____

_____

_____

_____

_____

_____

_____

_____

_____

Leadership and Servant-Leadership

A lot of times, especially as women, we try to please our partners by doing whatever it takes, even if it means changing ourselves entirely. But eventually, we reach a point where we can't keep up with it because we've lost sight of who we are. If you change everything about yourself just to fit into someone else's expectations, you're setting yourself up for frustration and imbalance.

Even though my husband Delroy is a great match for me, I had to remind myself, 'Hold on, I can't lose who I am in this.' Delroy is a soft, gentle person, and I'm naturally a more direct and assertive person—what you might call the 'honey-do' type. I'm always asking, 'Honey, can you do this? Honey, can you do that?' But I had to realize that trying to mold myself into someone I wasn't wouldn't work in the long run.

In a relationship, you have to come as your authentic self and stay true to your own standards. That's especially important in the dating phase. When you're dating, it's easy to think you have to be perfect or fit some ideal version of what you think your partner wants. But relationships aren't about two perfect people coming together; they're about two imperfect people learning to grow together. Compromise is essential.

If I hadn't learned how to compromise, I don't think Delroy and I would have made it. I'll admit I was bull-headed and determined to have my way early on. Delroy and I also come from very different family dynamics. He's seen how my family interacts, especially the couples, and he has pointed out that the women in my family tend not to respect men the way they should. He would make little comments like, '*That's why the marriages don't work in your family, because the women are too strong.*' As hard as it was to hear, there was truth in what he was saying, and it challenged me to reflect on my behavior and our dynamic.

Ultimately, I've learned that part of being supportive and respectful in marriage is recognizing where you need to grow and being willing to change— not to lose yourself, but to build a stronger foundation for the relationship. Allowing my husband to lead was something I was willing to do because he is a smart, dedicated, responsible, God-fearing man who seeks to lead with integrity. His leadership reminded me that true leadership in marriage isn't about domination, and my role was to support and facilitate his leadership.

For husbands, leading a marriage is not about asserting dominance or control. The Bible calls husbands to lead their wives as Christ leads the Church—with humility, selflessness, and relentless love, setting the tone for a partnership rooted in mutual respect and faith.. In a world that often equates leadership with power, biblical leadership is about servanthood. It is laying down one's life—emotionally, mentally, spiritually—for the betterment of the marriage and family.

- **Husbands as Servant-Leaders:** The call for husbands to lead is a heavy responsibility, not a privilege of control. Christ modeled leadership by washing the feet of His disciples, by enduring pain and suffering for the sake of those He loved. A husband must embody this servant-leadership, being willing to sacrifice his own desires, ambitions, and comfort to ensure that his wife and family are nurtured, protected, and spiritually fed.

- **Wives Supporting Leadership:** Supporting your husband's leadership isn't about blind obedience or silence; it's about creating an environment where he feels encouraged to lead with confidence in the Lord. It's about sharing wisdom, offering insight, and walking through difficult decisions together. The more you affirm his leadership, the more you cultivate an atmosphere where he can lead with humility and grace, knowing that he has your unwavering support.

REFLECT

In what ways do you feel society's view of submission conflicts with biblical submission? How do you reconcile these differences?

_____

_____

_____

_____

_____

_____

_____

_____

_____

_____

_____

_____

_____

_____

REFLECT

In what ways can you demonstrate submission as strength rather than weakness in your relationship?

_____

_____

_____

_____

_____

_____

_____

_____

_____

_____

_____

_____

_____

_____

Fortification Prayer

Lord, we seek Your guidance as we learn to submit to one another in love and humility. Help us embrace Your design for marriage, where wives support their husbands with strength and grace, and husbands lead with sacrificial love and humility, just as Christ leads the Church. Teach us to serve one another selflessly, and may our marriage reflect Your love and bring You glory.
In Jesus' name,
Amen

Work Out Your Faith:

Intentional Service

Activity: Over the next week, set aside intentional time each day to serve your spouse in a way that reflects Christ's love. Whether it's through small acts of kindness, words of encouragement, or simply listening without distraction, focus on ways to elevate and support each other.

At the end of each day, reflect on these moments by journaling your thoughts:

- How did serving your spouse make you feel?
- How did your spouse respond?
- In what ways did this act of service strengthen your connection?
- What did God reveal to you about your role in your marriage through this practice?

End of Week Reflection: After a week of serving, pray together, asking God to reveal how you can continue to grow in servant-leadership and mutual submission. Discuss the changes you noticed in your relationship and the ways you felt God working in your marriage.

BUILDING INTIMACY: EMOTIONAL, SPIRITUAL, & PHYSICAL

Intimacy in marriage is a gift from God that goes beyond the physical. It's about creating deep connections in all areas—spiritually, emotionally, and physically—that unite a husband and wife as one. A marriage built on intimacy fosters trust, security, and a bond that can withstand the storms of life. This section will explore how to build and nurture these three dimensions of intimacy in a Christ-centered marriage.

Spiritual Intimacy

Spiritual intimacy is the foundation upon which the rest of your marriage is built. Without a deep, shared relationship with God, everything else remains shallow. It is not enough to have individual relationships with Christ—true unity in marriage comes when you seek Him together. Spiritual intimacy draws both spouses toward a common purpose, helping you grow closer to each other as you grow closer to God.

Matthew 18:20 "For where two or three gather in my name, there am I with them."

When you and your spouse come together in prayer, worship, or studying Scripture, you are inviting the very presence of God into your marriage. His presence brings peace, guidance, and strength to weather any storm. Spiritual intimacy equips you to face the difficulties of life with a united front, knowing that your marriage is grounded in the one unshakable foundation—Christ. To cultivate this kind of closeness in my own relationship, I've learned a few key practices that have helped deepen my spiritual connection with my husband, and I'd like to share them with you.

Delroy has really empowered me to spend more time in the Word because he saw that it was in me, and he encouraged me to be around more Christian-minded people. He even wanted me to start getting more involved in church. Before we got married, we used to pray on the phone all the time. Once Delroy and I moved in together, things changed, though. I can't even tell you how many times we prayed after that—maybe two or three. It wasn't the same. We used to talk about the goodness of God all the time while dating, but once he started living with me, it felt different. He's told me many times that what drew him to me was my spirituality. When I called my mom to tell her I'd met someone just like her, who loved to pray together, she admired our connection.

I'll admit, I drop the ball at times on that, and even today, I'm still trying to get back to where I was when we were courting. Delroy can tell when I'm slipping, and he'll remind me, *"When are you going to pick up your Bible?"*

He holds me accountable. He tells me, *"You could get so much more from God if you were just more honest with yourself and stopped doing certain things."*

Building spiritual intimacy, like my journey with Delroy, requires openness, accountability, and a shared commitment to nurturing our faith. It's easy to become complacent once you get married, so developing spiritual intimacy while dating is important.

Ways to cultivate spiritual intimacy:

- **Daily prayer together**: It doesn't have to be long or complicated. Praying together every day fosters unity and builds a habit of bringing your concerns and hopes before God as a team.
- **Studying Scripture together**: Make time to read the Word as a couple, seeking God's wisdom for your marriage and discussing how His teachings can be applied to your relationship.
- **Spiritual accountability**: Hold each other accountable in your spiritual growth. Share what God is revealing to you individually, and encourage one another to grow closer to Him.

Spiritual intimacy doesn't happen by accident; it requires intentionality and vulnerability. But when a marriage is rooted in God's love and purpose, it becomes stronger and more resilient, able to withstand the trials and temptations that come your way.

REFLECT

How can you regularly check in with your partner to ensure that your spiritual intimacy is being nurtured and not neglected?

_____

_____

_____

_____

_____

_____

_____

_____

_____

_____

_____

_____

_____

_____

Emotional Intimacy

Emotional intimacy is the thread that weaves a couple's hearts together. It is built on trust, vulnerability, and the willingness to open yourself fully to your spouse, without fear of judgment or rejection. Without emotional connection, a marriage can feel empty, even if everything else seems "fine" on the surface. Emotional intimacy allows you to experience the deep companionship God intended when He said, "It is not good for man to be alone" **(Genesis 2:18).**

In the Song of Solomon, we see a beautiful picture of emotional intimacy between lovers who are open and transparent with one another. They express their admiration, fears, and desires with deep vulnerability, creating a bond that goes beyond physical attraction. True emotional intimacy requires that same level of openness, where both spouses feel safe to share their deepest thoughts and feelings.

Building emotional intimacy requires:

- **Honest communication**: Share your fears, dreams, and struggles with your spouse. Be vulnerable, even when it feels uncomfortable. Deep emotional connection can only happen when both partners are willing to be fully known.
- **Active listening**: Be present and attentive when your spouse speaks. Listening is not just hearing words but understanding the heart behind them.
- **Showing empathy**: Meet your spouse where they are emotionally. Validate their feelings, and offer support rather than solutions when they're going through difficult times.

Emotional intimacy grows over time as you both learn to trust each other more deeply. It creates a safe space in your marriage, where both partners feel secure, loved, and valued. It is the foundation of a strong marriage built on trust, vulnerability, and openness. It enables couples to connect deeply, as seen in the Song of Solomon, where lovers share their fears, desires, and admiration, creating a bond beyond physical attraction and fulfilling God's design for companionship.

REFLECT

How can you actively create a safe and open space in your relationship to share emotions, deepen trust, and reflect Christ's love in your connection with your partner?

_____

_____

_____

_____

_____

_____

_____

_____

_____

_____

_____

_____

Physical Intimacy: The Gift of Sex in Marriage

Physical intimacy is often reduced to mere physical pleasure, but in the context of marriage, it is so much more. God designed sex to be an expression of love, trust, and oneness between husband and wife. It is a sacred gift that mirrors the vulnerability, passion, and selflessness found in a relationship with God. When physical intimacy is treated as a holy expression of love, it becomes a powerful way to strengthen the bond between husband and wife.

1 Corinthians 7:3-5 tells us, "The husband should fulfill his marital duty to his wife, and likewise the wife to her husband... Do not deprive each other except by mutual consent and for a time, so that you may devote yourselves to prayer."

This scripture emphasizes the importance of maintaining physical intimacy in marriage, not as an obligation but as a mutual act of love and connection. Neglecting this area of your marriage can open the door to temptation and disconnection, but when nurtured with love and respect, physical intimacy becomes a life-giving expression of unity.

Key aspects of building healthy physical intimacy include:

- Communicating your needs: Physical intimacy thrives when both partners are open about their desires and boundaries. Silence and assumption create distance; honest communication fosters deeper connection.

- Making time for intimacy: In the busyness of life, physical intimacy can sometimes be overlooked. Make it a priority, recognizing that it is a vital part of a healthy, God-honoring marriage.

- Viewing sex as worship: Physical intimacy in marriage is not just a physical act; it's a reflection of the love and selflessness that Christ has for the church. When approached with reverence and gratitude, it can become a form of worship to God.

Physical intimacy is not something to be taken lightly or neglected. When viewed through the lens of God's design, it becomes a vital part of the marriage that brings joy, connection, and a deeper sense of unity.

REFLECT

How can you cultivate a mindset that views physical intimacy as a reflection of Christ's love for the church, making it more meaningful and worshipful in your marriage?

_____

_____

_____

_____

_____

_____

_____

_____

_____

_____

_____

_____

Fortification Prayer

Lord, we invite You to be the center of every aspect of our intimacy. Help us to deepen our spiritual connection with You first, that it may overflow into our marriage. Teach us to be vulnerable with one another, just as You were vulnerable in Your love for us. Give us the courage to open up emotionally, sharing our hearts and listening with empathy. Guide us to honor and cherish physical intimacy as a gift from You, fostering connection and mutual respect. May our love for one another reflect Your love for us, growing stronger in every season. In Jesus' name, Amen.

Work Out Your Faith:

Check In

Set aside intentional, uninterrupted time each week to conduct a Marriage Intimacy Check-In. Create a safe space where you and your spouse can openly discuss your spiritual, emotional, and physical connection.

1. **Spiritual Check-In**: Share how you feel about your walk with God and pray together for guidance in strengthening your spiritual bond as a couple. Consider starting a new devotional or scripture-reading habit together.
2. **Emotional Check-In**: Take turns expressing any unspoken emotional needs, concerns, or desires. Listen without interruption or judgment. Offer support and discuss ways to better connect emotionally during the upcoming week.
3. **Physical Check-In**: Have a healthy, respectful conversation about your physical intimacy. This is an opportunity to share any feelings, thoughts, or changes you'd like to make in this area. The goal is to ensure both partners feel loved, respected, and understood.

INSIGHT

Use this area to write additional insights from the readings, reflection questions or activity responses.

_____

_____

_____

_____

_____

_____

_____

_____

_____

_____

_____

_____

_____

OVERCOMING CHALLENGES IN MARRIAGE

Marriage, no matter how strong or centered on God, will face challenges. These obstacles aren't meant to destroy the relationship but to refine it, drawing both partners closer to each other and to God. In this section, we will explore practical, biblical strategies for handling conflict, forgiving one another, and balancing expectations with reality.

Handling Conflict Biblically

Conflict is inevitable in marriage, but how we respond to it determines whether it brings us closer or creates division. The Bible provides clear guidance on handling disagreements with wisdom, grace, and love.

James 1:19-20 "My dear brothers and sisters, take note of this: Everyone should be quick to listen, slow to speak and slow to become angry, because human anger does not produce the righteousness that God desires."

These verses encourage us to listen actively, hold back impulsive words, and exercise patience. In marriage, this means approaching conflict with an open heart, seeking to understand your spouse's perspective rather than simply defending your own position. Anger clouds judgment and fuels division. To handle conflict biblically:

- **Pause and Pray**: Before reacting, take a moment to pray, asking God for wisdom and peace.
- **Communicate with Love**: Approach your spouse with a gentle, loving spirit. Instead of attacking, express how you feel without placing blame.
- **Seek Understanding**: Focus on truly understanding your spouse's point of view before sharing your own.
- **Stay Solution-Oriented**: Once emotions settle, work to find a compromise or solution that honors both of you and aligns with God's Word.

When handled this way, conflict doesn't have to tear you apart; it can actually strengthen your bond as you practice humility and forgiveness.

REFLECT

How does your current or future husband feel most loved and understood during times of disagreement? How can you better support him and communicate love even when you don't see eye-to-eye?

_____

_____

_____

_____

_____

_____

_____

_____

_____

_____

_____

_____

_____

_____

Forgiveness in Marriage

Forgiveness is at the heart of every healthy marriage. Without it, resentment builds, and hearts harden. Jesus emphasized the power of forgiveness when He said:

Matthew 6:14-15 " For if you forgive other people when they sin against you, your heavenly Father will also forgive you. But if you do not forgive others their sins, your Father will not forgive your sins."

In marriage, we must continually offer forgiveness, just as Christ has forgiven us. Forgiveness does not mean excusing hurtful behavior or ignoring issues. It means releasing the right to hold grudges and trusting God to heal what has been broken.

Some steps toward forgiveness in marriage include:

- **Acknowledge the Hurt**: Forgiveness begins with acknowledging the pain or offense.

- **Pray for Healing**: Ask God to heal your heart and give you the strength to forgive, even when it's difficult.

- **Choose to Let Go**: Forgiveness is a decision, not a feeling. Choose to let go of bitterness and trust God's justice.

- **Rebuild Trust**: While forgiveness is given freely, rebuilding trust takes time. Allow space for growth and restoration.

Forgiveness is vital for creating a lasting union. It allows love to flourish and reflects God's grace in your marriage.

REFLECT

Are you holding onto past disappointments in your relationship? How can you let go and trust God to bring healing and restoration?

_____

_____

_____

_____

_____

_____

_____

_____

_____

_____

_____

_____

Balancing Expectations vs. Reality

Every marriage brings with it expectations—personal, cultural, or even societal. Sometimes, these expectations clash with reality, leaving couples frustrated or disappointed.

Proverbs 13:12 "Hope deferred makes the heart sick, but a longing fulfilled is a tree of life."

It's easy to place unrealistic expectations on our spouse, expecting them to fulfill all our emotional, physical, and spiritual needs. However, no human can meet all these demands—only God can. Marriage is not about perfect fulfillment but about learning to love each other despite imperfections.

Here are practical steps for balancing expectations with reality:
- **Adjust Expectations**: Understand that your spouse is human, with flaws and limitations. Instead of focusing on what they lack, appreciate the qualities they do bring.

- **Communicate Needs Clearly**: Don't assume your spouse knows what you need. Open, honest communication is key to aligning expectations with reality.

- **Release Unrealistic Ideals**: Society often places unattainable ideals on marriage, from social media highlight reels to unrealistic portrayals of relationships. Release these false comparisons and focus on the unique journey God has for your marriage.

- **Prioritize Grace and Love**: When expectations go unmet, extend grace and patience. Love is not about having your expectations met at every turn, but about choosing to stay committed and supportive even in challenging times.

REFLECT

How can you guard your heart against comparing your relationship or marriage to others? How can you cultivate contentment in what God has blessed you with?

_____

_____

_____

_____

_____

_____

_____

_____

_____

_____

_____

_____

_____

Fortification Prayer

Lord, we ask for Your wisdom and grace to guide us as we navigate challenges in our marriage. Help us to handle conflict with patience and love, seeking to understand rather than to be understood. Teach us to forgive as You forgive, freeing our hearts from bitterness and resentment. When expectations fall short, help us to extend grace to one another and trust Your purpose for our marriage. May our union reflect Your love and bring glory to Your name.
In Jesus' name,
Amen

Work Out Your Faith:

Strengthening Through Challenges

Activity:
- **Reflect and Reframe:**
  - Take a moment to write down one recent conflict or challenge you've faced in your marriage. Describe how it made you feel and what outcome you hoped for.
  - Now, reframe the situation by identifying how this challenge might be an opportunity for growth, unity, or deeper reliance on God. Write a few sentences on what you learned or how you can view the challenge differently.
  -

- **Pray Together:**
  - Set aside time to pray with your spouse specifically about your challenges. Ask God for wisdom, patience, and a spirit of unity. If praying together feels difficult, start by praying individually for one another and then come together to share your prayers.

Activity: • **Forgiveness Exercise:**
  ○ Reflect on any unresolved hurts.
    Ask yourself: "Am I holding onto
    something that could hinder our
    unity?" Write down what you need
    to forgive or seek forgiveness for.
    Then, share this with your spouse in
    a loving, non-confrontational way,
    focusing on reconciliation.

• **Expectations Inventory:**
  ○ Write down three expectations you
    have for your marriage. Discuss
    these with your spouse, asking: "Are
    these expectations realistic? How
    can we align them with God's vision
    for our relationship?"

• **Scripture Meditation:**
  ○ Choose a verse related to
    overcoming challenges or unity in
    marriage (e.g., Ephesians 4:2-3).
    Meditate on this verse together and
    discuss how it can guide your
    approach to handling future
    obstacles.

By completing this activity, you'll deepen
your understanding of how challenges can
refine your relationship, equipping you to
face them with grace, faith, and unity.

INSIGHT

Use this area to write additional insights from the readings, reflection questions or activity responses.

_____

_____

_____

_____

_____

_____

_____

_____

_____

_____

_____

_____

_____

_____

UNITY IN PURPOSE & CALLING

When two people come together in marriage, it's not only the merging of hearts but also the blending of individual callings and purposes. The beauty of a Christ-centered marriage is that it becomes more than just a relationship; it becomes a divine partnership aimed at fulfilling God's kingdom purposes. This section explores the power of unity in purpose and how husbands and wives can support each other in their unique callings, while moving forward together in God's plans.

Discovering Your Shared Purpose

One of the most profound aspects of marriage is discovering how God has uniquely equipped both you and your husband to serve His kingdom together. A marriage rooted in Christ doesn't only focus on personal happiness but on fulfilling a higher purpose. God has joined you for more than companionship —He has a kingdom assignment for your marriage.

Look at the example of Priscilla and Aquila in the New Testament. This couple is mentioned multiple times throughout the book of Acts and Paul's letters. They worked together in ministry, spreading the gospel and even hosting a church in their home (Acts 18:1-3, 24-26). Their unity in purpose allowed them to make a significant impact in the early church. Priscilla and Aquila shared a deep partnership, one in which they strengthened each other and advanced God's kingdom side by side.

Acts 18:24-26 shows how this couple worked together to disciple Apollos, a young preacher, teaching him more accurately about the ways of God. Their influence in the church was powerful because they united in mission, encouraging and uplifting each other along the way.

In your marriage, discovering your shared purpose may not happen all at once, but it begins with seeking God together in prayer and asking Him how He wants to use your marriage. What passions or burdens has He placed on both of your hearts? What gifts and talents can you use together to serve others and build His kingdom?

REFLECT

What values, passions, or goals do you and your spouse share, and how can you work together to build a unified purpose that honors both your individual callings and your relationship?

_____

_____

_____

_____

_____

_____

_____

_____

_____

_____

_____

_____

_____

_____

Supporting Each Other's Individual Callings

While marriage unites two people in a shared purpose, it's important to recognize that each person in the relationship has a unique calling from God. Supporting each other's individual callings is an essential part of building a strong, Christ-centered marriage. Marriage doesn't mean losing your identity or the distinct gifts God has given you—it means creating space for both of you to flourish and live out your divine purpose.

In the same way that Priscilla and Aquila supported each other, you are called to lift up your husband in his calling while also pursuing your own. It's a delicate balance, but it is possible to maintain unity while also encouraging each other to thrive in your individual assignments from God.

For example, you may have a calling to teach or lead within your church or community, while your husband may feel called to business or missions. In these cases, supporting each other might look like making sacrifices for one another, offering encouragement, and creating time for both of you to invest in these areas. This kind of support requires humility, love, and constant communication.

Think of the example of Esther, who was called to a specific role as queen to save her people. Her husband, King Xerxes, supported her in this, even though her calling was distinct from his role. Her courage and wisdom in fulfilling her God-given mission allowed her to make a tremendous impact. Likewise, your husband may have a calling that requires you to adjust your own schedule or plans at times, but when both people are committed to supporting each other in their God-given callings, the result is a stronger, more unified marriage.

Ecclesiastes 4:9 "Two are better than one because they have a good return for their labor."

Couples can actively encourage and uplift each other by being each other's biggest cheerleader. Offer words of affirmation, celebrate milestones, and provide emotional support during challenges. They can also collaborate and share skills, using their unique strengths to complement each other's calling. If one partner is great with organization and the other excels at public speaking, combine those talents to build something together, such as hosting workshops.

REFLECT

How are you currently supporting your partner or spouse in his purpose or calling, and what more can you do to actively contribute to their journey?

_____

_____

_____

_____

_____

_____

_____

_____

_____

_____

_____

_____

_____

REFLECT

Are there any areas where you've felt competition with your future or current husband's calling? How can you release that and focus on mutual support?

_____

_____

_____

_____

_____

_____

_____

_____

_____

_____

_____

_____

_____

_____

Walking in Unity Together

I believe a husband should actively support his wife's purpose or calling, whether by joining her efforts directly or by standing behind her in encouragement. What's crucial is that he never undermines her journey. In my case, my husband is deeply authentic and would only join me if he saw God's hand in my work and my life reflecting true integrity.

For instance, if Delroy noticed me engaging in behaviors that didn't align with Christian values, like going back to the casino, he wouldn't support me ministering to women about relationships at a Christian conference. He simply isn't a hypocrite, and he expects the same from me. That accountability has helped me evaluate myself, identifying areas I need to address privately before stepping into public ministry.

In general, I think it's vital for spouses to be part of each other's journey in fulfilling their callings. If they're not, it can leave a void. For me, having Delroy join me in my purpose is essential—it completes the fulfillment of what I'm called to do. His strong values and authenticity add depth to the partnership we share, making the journey richer and more meaningful."

Ultimately, your marriage is not just about two individuals, but about the way God can use both of you together to accomplish more for His kingdom than either of you could alone. A Christ-centered marriage is one where you not only love and support each other but where you unite in purpose to be instruments of God's love and grace in the world.

Fulfilling God's will should be the ultimate goal in everything you do, including your relationships. If your relationship goals don't align with your calling, something will inevitably suffer. That's why it's so important to ensure your partnership is working toward the same purpose.

In recent years, it's become more common to see pastors' wives actively serving as their husbands' assistants in church and ministry. This reflects the idea that if two people can't walk together in unity, they won't be able to fully realize God's purpose. Alignment is essential—not just for success, but for harmony and fulfillment in both your relationship and calling.

As you and your husband grow in your relationship with God, your marriage will reflect the beauty of His design and the fullness of His plans for both of you.

REFLECT

Have you ever struggled with balancing your individual calling and your shared purpose? What steps can you take to find harmony between the two?

_____

_____

_____

_____

_____

_____

_____

_____

_____

_____

_____

_____

_____

REFLECT

Are there any areas where your personal goals or habits might unintentionally hinder your partner's ability to fulfill his purpose? How can you align your actions to better support him and walk in unity?

_____

_____

_____

_____

_____

_____

_____

_____

_____

_____

_____

_____

Fortification Prayer

Heavenly Father, we come before You with humble hearts, grateful for the gift of marriage and the divine partnership it represents. Thank You for uniting two lives not only in love but in purpose, creating a bond that reflects Your glory and fulfills Your kingdom plans. Lord, help us to see our marriage as more than a union of two hearts but as a blending of the unique callings and purposes You have placed within us.

Strengthen us, Lord, to support one another wholeheartedly, to celebrate each other's gifts, and to walk forward in unity, trusting Your guidance. Where there may be differences, grant us understanding; where there may be challenges, fill us with grace. Bind us together with a shared vision for the future, rooted in Your will and led by Your Spirit.

May our marriage be a beacon of light to others, demonstrating the beauty of a Christ-centered union and the power of moving forward in unity. Use us, Lord, as vessels to further Your kingdom and leave a legacy of faith, love, and purpose.

In Jesus' name,

Amen

Work Out Your Faith:

Aligning in Purpose and Calling

Activity:

Step 1: Pray Together

Set aside time to pray as a couple. Ask God to reveal His purpose for your marriage and to guide both of you in understanding how your individual callings align with His greater plan.

Step 2: Reflect and Share

Individually, take 10–15 minutes to reflect on the following questions and write down your thoughts before sharing them:

- What do you believe God has called you to do in this season of life?
- How do you see your gifts and talents contributing to God's kingdom?
- How do you feel your marriage can glorify God and make an impact?
- How can you combine your individual callings to serve a greater purpose together?

Write down a mission statement for your marriage that reflects your shared purpose, such as: *"Our marriage exists to honor God by serving others, growing in faith, and supporting each other in fulfilling His plan."*

Step 4: Create a Support Plan

Brainstorm ways to actively support each other's individual callings.

BUILDING A LEGACY TOGETHER

Marriage is not just about the here and now—it's about creating something lasting, a legacy that will endure beyond your lifetime. A Christ-centered marriage has the power to impact future generations, shaping not only your own lives but also the lives of your children, your community, and even people you may never meet. The legacy you and your husband build together, grounded in faith, is one that can leave an eternal imprint on your family and the world around you.

Leaving a Legacy of Faith

A legacy of faith begins with a deep commitment to God and each other. It is about passing down the values, principles, and beliefs that have shaped your life in Christ to those who will come after you. In Deuteronomy 6:6-7, God instructs His people to embed His words into their hearts and to diligently teach them to their children. This principle of training the next generation in the ways of the Lord is at the heart of leaving a legacy of faith.

Deuteronomy 6:6-7 "These commandments that I give you today are to be on your hearts. Impress them on your children. Talk about them when you sit at home and when you walk along the road, when you lie down and when you get up."

Building a legacy together starts with nurturing your marriage in such a way that it becomes a testimony of God's grace, love, and faithfulness. The example you set as husband and wife is one of the most powerful tools for passing down faith. Your children, family members, and even those who witness your marriage will learn about God by the way you honor, love, and serve each other. This is how your marriage becomes a living testimony of Christ's love for the church.

This legacy extends beyond words; it's about modeling Christlike behavior in every aspect of your lives. When your children see you and your husband praying together, serving others, and facing trials with faith, they are learning to do the same. When they see you forgive each other, show grace, and remain committed in difficult times, they learn what it means to walk in faithfulness.

Your legacy is not only spiritual; it's relational as well, and this includes finances. My husband, Delroy, also had an issue with how I managed my finances. Whenever someone needed something, they would call me, and no matter my own financial situation, I'd find a way to help them. Growing up, my mother was always a financial lifeline for me, and I saw myself as generous, just like her. There was a major difference, however; my mother was financially responsible because my father kept a close eye on their budget and spending.

I, on the other hand, was carefree with money. I loved shopping and ended up accumulating significant credit card debt. Even so, I continued to help friends and family when they faced financial difficulties. One time, Delroy confronted me about this habit. He said, "You're not here to please everyone, and you're not Jesus Christ. Why do you feel the need to help every time someone calls?"

I'll never forget one instance in particular. My friend's daughter called and asked me to pay for her passport so she could travel to Jamaica. Without hesitation, I agreed. Then, after I'd already committed to covering the cost of the passport, they asked me for spending money for the trip as well. When I told Delroy, he was furious. He couldn't believe I had made such a decision without considering our financial priorities.

That moment was a wake-up call. I realized that while being generous is admirable, it can't come at the expense of financial stability or the goals we were trying to achieve together as a couple. Delroy helped me see that building a legacy required discipline, responsibility, and clear priorities.

I had to take a hard look at my spending habits and make changes to ensure our financial health wasn't jeopardized. Supporting others is important, but it must be done in a way that aligns with the bigger picture—establishing a strong financial foundation and legacy for our future.

Your marriage can set the tone for how your children and others in your life will approach their own relationships, teaching them the importance of love, commitment, and selflessness. The investment you make in building a strong, faith-filled marriage will ripple through your family for years to come. Leaving a legacy of healthy, God-centered relationships can change the course of future generations.

REFLECT

What sacrifices are you willing to make now to ensure a lasting legacy for your family's future?

_____

_____

_____

_____

_____

_____

_____

_____

_____

_____

_____

_____

Raising Children in Faith

If God blesses your marriage with children, one of the most significant parts of your legacy will be how you raise them. While the world is constantly pulling children in different directions, your home can be a sanctuary where they learn about God's love and purpose for their lives. Deuteronomy 6 emphasizes the importance of teaching your children about God in the everyday moments of life—when you're at home, when you're traveling, when you wake up, and when you go to bed.

To leave a lasting legacy of faith for your children, you must first cultivate your own relationship with God. Children learn by example, and the most effective way to teach them about God is by living out your faith authentically. This means showing them what it looks like to trust God in difficult times, to forgive when it's hard, and to serve others with humility. It also means creating rhythms of spiritual practices in your home, such as reading the Bible together, praying as a family, and worshiping God together.

My husband and I have a blended family, and we have sought to unite in faith. In a blended family, which includes stepparents, it's important for everyone to learn how to co-parent and get along for the sake of the child. I believe it's crucial not to exclude your spouse from the relationship with your child(ren), especially if he wants to be involved in the child's life. You must find a way to make it work, or it could signal deeper issues in the marriage. I see this dynamic every day in my work as a school administrator. Often, I observe that when a new husband enters the picture, there's a tendency to exclude the biological father or vice versa. A new husband must be supportive and allow space for the biological parent to fulfill his role. Even if the relationship with the exs is challenging, it's not healthy to pretend the other parent doesn't exist.

Even if the biological father has "issues," a child will idolize him more in his absence. Thus, acknowledging the reality of the other parent's role is crucial. If there's significant conflict with an ex, perhaps it's best to wait before marrying, or at least until the child is older. Blended families can be complex, but being honest about the dynamics of all parties involved is key, especially when setting a Godly example of unity, peace and faith.

Raising children in faith is not just about teaching them religious practices; it's about showing them how to live out their faith in every area of life. Encourage them to develop their own relationship with God, to seek His guidance, and to understand their unique purpose in His kingdom.

REFLECT

How can your marriage serve as an example of Christ's love to your extended family, church, and community?

_____

_____

_____

_____

_____

_____

_____

_____

_____

_____

_____

_____

Building a Godly Family Foundation

A Christ-centered legacy is built on the foundation of a godly family. Whether or not you have children, you and your husband can create a family culture that honors God. This involves making intentional decisions about how you will spend your time, use your resources, and approach challenges together. Consider the ways you can build a godly family foundation by serving others, opening your home for hospitality, and being involved in your church and community. Your marriage has the potential to be a beacon of light, not just for your immediate family but for those who observe how you live out your faith. When others see the peace, love, and joy that flows from your marriage, they will be drawn to Christ through your example.

God's purpose for your marriage goes beyond your personal happiness; it's about glorifying Him and advancing His kingdom through the legacy you leave. Whether you are raising children, mentoring others, or simply living out your faith in the everyday, your marriage is a vehicle for His glory. To achieve this, here are some tips for building a Godly family foundation:

- **Make God the Center of Your Home**: Model a Christ-centered life by prioritizing prayer, worship, and studying the Bible together as a family. Create a culture where seeking God's guidance is the first response to challenges and decisions.

- **Teach the Word Early and Often**: Introduce your children to God's Word at a young age and help them understand its principles. Memorize scripture as a family and discuss its application in everyday life.

- **Lead by Example**: Children learn more from what they see than what they're told. Let them witness your faith in action through your love for God, your spouse, and others. Show forgiveness, humility, and grace in your daily interactions.

- **Prioritize Family Prayer Time:** Develop the habit of praying together daily. Let your children hear you thanking God, asking for His guidance, and lifting up others. Prayer strengthens bonds and teaches reliance on God in all circumstances.

- **Pass Down Stories of Faith**: Share testimonies of how God has worked in your life and the lives of your ancestors. Hearing stories of God's faithfulness inspires trust and encourages perseverance in their own spiritual journeys.

- **Instill Values of Service and Stewardship**: Teach your children to serve others with love and generosity. Involve them in acts of kindness, whether volunteering at church, helping a neighbor, or supporting charitable causes, to instill a heart of compassion.

- **Foster Open Communication**: Create a safe space where your children feel comfortable discussing their questions, doubts, and experiences about faith. Guide them with biblical wisdom while encouraging their spiritual growth.

- **Celebrate Milestones with Meaning**: Mark significant events in your children's spiritual journey, such as baptisms or mission trips, with celebrations that highlight the importance of their faith.

- **Encourage Accountability and Discipleship**: Teach your children the importance of surrounding themselves with like-minded believers who can encourage their walk with Christ. Help them find a mentor or discipleship group for additional support.

- **Plan for a Spiritual Legacy**: Leave a legacy that goes beyond material possessions by investing in your children's spiritual inheritance. Create traditions of faith, like family devotionals, and set the example of living with eternity in mind.

By intentionally building a godly family foundation, you create a legacy of faith that will impact generations to come.

REFLECT

What family legacy do you want to leave behind, and how does that align with God's vision for your life and marriage?

_____

_____

_____

_____

_____

_____

_____

_____

_____

_____

_____

_____

REFLECT

What specific steps can you take today to ensure that your family is or will be centered on God's Word and values, leaving a legacy of faith for future generations?

_____

_____

_____

_____

_____

_____

_____

_____

_____

_____

_____

_____

_____

Fortification Prayer

Heavenly Father, thank You for the blessing of my marriage and the purpose You've placed in our union. Help us to build a legacy that honors You, rooted in love, faith, and devotion to Your Word. Guide us as we raise future generations to know You, and let our lives reflect Your grace and truth. Strengthen us to live in unity, fulfilling the call You've placed on our lives, and may our love inspire others for years to come.
In Jesus' name,
Amen

Work Out Your Faith:

Create a Legacy Plan

Activity: Sit down with your partner and make a list of the values and principles you want to pass down to future generations. Discuss how you can intentionally live out those values in your marriage and family. Identify ways you can serve together, whether in your church, community, or even in mentoring other couples. Pray together for God's guidance on how to build a lasting legacy of faith.

Legacy-Focused Financial Plan
Answer the following questions:
1. What are my biggest spending triggers (e.g., shopping, dining out)?
2. Have I ever spent money that I couldn't afford to give away or didn't align with our family's goals or future?
3. What emotions drive my financial decisions (e.g., guilt, generosity, fear)?

For the next 30 days, record every expense in a notebook or app. Afterward, review your spending with your partner. Determine how you can support each other's financial weaknesses?

Write down your shared financial goals and post them somewhere visible as a reminder.

INSIGHT

Use this area to write additional insights from the readings, reflection questions or activity responses.

PROTECTING YOUR MARRIAGE

Just like anything of great value, your marriage requires intentional protection. We may not often think of marriage as something to guard, but it is uniquely shaped by the interactions and influences of extended family, friends, and even co-workers. These relationships, while important, can unintentionally interfere with your marriage if boundaries are not established. For example, a demanding boss accustomed to your late hours or "anytime" availability before marriage may need to adjust expectations once you're married. Similarly, close friends or buddies may need to understand that your priorities have shifted, and your time with them will become more limited. Additionally, unresolved emotions or bitterness from past relationships must not be allowed to linger and affect your current marriage. Protecting your marriage involves identifying these potential challenges and taking proactive steps to safeguard the bond you share.

Guarding Your Heart

The Bible gives us a powerful instruction in Proverbs 4:23: "Above all else, guard your heart, for everything you do flows from it." This verse is a reminder that your heart is the wellspring of your life, and what you allow into it shapes the health of your marriage. In the sacred covenant of marriage, guarding your heart is crucial because external temptations can seep into even the strongest relationships and erode the unity God has blessed.

Temptations can come in many forms—emotional, spiritual, or physical. These aren't always obvious sins; they might start as small distractions, seemingly harmless interactions, or even negative thought patterns that slowly chip away at the foundation of your relationship. A passing glance, an inappropriate conversation, or lingering feelings of frustration can be gateways for temptation. These seemingly minor cracks, if left unaddressed, can open the door to deeper, more destructive behaviors, such as emotional infidelity, a wandering heart, or resentment.

Jesus warned us to be vigilant, as the enemy prowls like a lion seeking whom he may devour **(1 Peter 5:8)**. In marriage, this vigilance is paramount.

Guarding your heart is not just about avoiding sin but about filling your heart with things that strengthen your marriage. What are you allowing to influence your thoughts and emotions? Are you feeding your heart with God's Word, love, and truth? Or are you opening it to comparison, frustration, or worldly desires?

These are some tips to help you guard your heart:

- **Daily Prayer and Devotion** – Stay connected to God as the source of your strength and wisdom. Ask Him to guard your heart and protect your marriage.

- **Open Communication** – Regularly talk about your emotional and spiritual health. Be transparent about any challenges you face so that you can support each other.

- **Accountability** – Have godly mentors or a support system who can help hold you accountable, whether it's for your thoughts, actions, or any temptations that arise.

- **Limit Harmful Influences** – Be mindful of the things you allow to influence you—whether it's entertainment, certain friendships, or conversations that don't build up your marriage.

- **Discern Emotional Boundaries** – Be cautious of how you emotionally invest in others outside your marriage. Emotional intimacy should be reserved for your spouse, and over-investing in others can lead to temptation.

Guarding your heart is an ongoing act of devotion, not only to your spouse but, more importantly, to God. As you submit your heart to Him daily, He will help you identify areas where you are vulnerable and give you the strength to resist any temptation that may arise. When you guard your heart, you safeguard the love and commitment in your marriage, allowing God to reign over your union.

REFLECT

Are there any emotional attachments or relationships outside your marriage that you need to reevaluate or create boundaries for?

_____

_____

_____

_____

_____

_____

_____

_____

_____

_____

_____

_____

_____

Setting Healthy Boundaries in Marriage

When I first got engaged to my husband, he had a significant issue with the number of friends I kept around me, particularly the women. Many of them weren't married, and some of their behaviors didn't align with the values he felt were necessary to protect our marriage. One friend in particular stood out as a concern for him. From the start, Delroy made it clear that she couldn't remain in my life. She was dating a married man, and for Delroy, that was completely unacceptable. I wasn't shocked by his reaction—I was embarrassed. He discovered early in our relationship that she was involved in an affair, and it bothered him deeply. He would question how someone like me, who held myself to high moral standards, could surround myself with people who made choices so contrary to those values. He felt strongly that my circle of friends needed to reflect the integrity and priorities of a married woman.

For Delroy, it wasn't just about me having friends—it was about the type of influence those friends could have on our relationship. He believed strongly in protecting the sanctity of our marriage, and that required making difficult decisions about who I allowed to stay in my inner circle. Looking back, I understand that he wasn't trying to control me; he was trying to create a safe and healthy foundation for our relationship.

Establishing boundaries in marriage is an essential practice to protect your relationship from external influences and distractions that could harm the intimacy and unity God intends for you and your spouse. While love is the core of marriage, boundaries are like the protective walls that ensure love grows and thrives without being trampled or invaded by outside pressures.

Boundaries aren't just about saying no to sin—they're about prioritizing what matters most: the relationship between you, your spouse, and God. Without boundaries, it's easy for well-meaning people or things to consume the time and energy that should be devoted to your spouse. Whether it's a friend who monopolizes your attention, a work schedule that leaves little room for connection, or even family members who don't respect the sanctity of your marriage, boundaries help maintain the sacredness of your relationship.

Key Areas to Set Boundaries:
- **Friends and Family**:
  While maintaining relationships with friends and family is important, it's

essential to establish limits to protect your marriage. Sometimes, family and friends can unintentionally overstep, offering opinions or expecting time that interferes with your marriage. Setting healthy boundaries ensures that your spouse always knows they come first. This also includes limiting involvement in conflicts or decisions that should remain between you and your spouse.

- **Technology and Social Media:**
 In today's digital age, it's easy to let technology steal moments of intimacy and quality time with your spouse. Phones, computers, and social media can create invisible walls if you allow them to replace meaningful connection. Set boundaries on how much screen time is allowed during shared moments, such as mealtime or before bed. Be intentional about spending time offline to cultivate closeness and deeper conversations with your spouse.

- **Work-Life Balance:**
 Balancing work and home life is another area where boundaries must be set. Many marriages suffer when one or both spouses are overworked, leading to exhaustion, frustration, and little time for nurturing the relationship. Setting boundaries around work ensures that neither spouse is neglected, and it allows both partners to prioritize each other's emotional and physical needs.

- **Emotional Boundaries with Others:**
 Creating emotional boundaries with others is crucial to protect the deep intimacy that only belongs to your marriage. Confiding in others about personal struggles with your spouse, or sharing emotionally vulnerable moments, can create opportunities for temptation or emotional dependency. It's essential to reserve your most intimate thoughts, feelings, and concerns for your spouse and avoid any situation where a bond with someone else could challenge the unity of your marriage.

- **Spiritual Boundaries:**
 Finally, spiritual boundaries are necessary to ensure your marriage remains centered on God. Prioritize your spiritual growth together, being careful not to let other distractions come between you and your walk with the Lord as a couple. Setting boundaries with time, commitments, and spiritual practices can help ensure that you both you continue to grow closer to God.

Practical Tips for Setting Boundaries:

- Have open conversations with your spouse about areas in your life where you feel boundaries are needed. Be transparent about what you both need to feel safe, respected, and prioritized.
- Be proactive rather than reactive. Don't wait for problems to arise—set boundaries before outside influences cause friction in your relationship.
- Stand firm in your boundaries even if others don't understand or agree. What matters most is protecting your marriage and the love God has given you to nurture.

When you set healthy boundaries in your marriage, you create a space where your relationship can flourish, free from unnecessary conflict or distractions. Boundaries allow both partners to feel safe, valued, and cherished, ensuring that God's design for your marriage remains the priority.

REFLECT

How have external influences—social media, work, family—affected your ability to prioritize your spouse and your marriage? What steps can you take to minimize their influence?

_____

_____

_____

_____

_____

_____

_____

_____

_____

_____

_____

_____

_____

REFLECT

How can you cultivate a deeper awareness of the enemy's tactics to create division and temptation in your marriage?

_____

_____

_____

_____

_____

_____

_____

_____

_____

_____

_____

_____

Fortification Prayer

Lord, I come before You with a heart open to Your guidance and protection. I know that my marriage is a sacred covenant, and I ask for Your wisdom in guarding my heart against any temptations or distractions that could harm it. Help me to be vigilant and intentional in protecting the unity You've created between my spouse and me. Give me the strength to set boundaries where they are needed and the grace to uphold them with love.

Teach me to communicate openly with my spouse and to honor the intimacy we share by keeping it sacred, free from external interference. I ask that You be the center of our marriage, that Your Word and Spirit will guide us as we grow closer to each other and to You.

Father, I ask that You keep our hearts aligned with Your will, so we may resist the pull of the world and focus on what truly matters: honoring You in our love for one another. Help us build a marriage that reflects Your love, rooted in faith, grace, and unwavering commitment.

In Jesus' name,

Amen

Work Out Your Faith:

Building a Fortress Around Your Marriage

Activity: **Step 1: Personal Reflection**

Ask yourself the following questions:

- What habits, relationships, or activities in my life could potentially distract me from prioritizing my marriage?
- Are there unresolved emotions, such as bitterness or hurt from past experiences, that might affect my relationship?
- What steps can I take to ensure my heart remains focused on nurturing my marriage and honoring my spouse?

After writing down your responses, pray or meditate on your answers, asking for clarity and wisdom to guard your heart against anything that might hinder your marriage.

Step 2: Joint Discussion

As a couple, discuss the following areas where boundaries might be needed:

- Workplace: How can we ensure work responsibilities or colleagues do not encroach on our personal time together?
- Friendships: Are there any friendships that need to be redefined to protect our marriage?
- Family: How do we handle extended family dynamics to maintain unity in our relationship?

86

Activity:
- Social Media & Technology: What boundaries should we set to ensure that technology supports rather than detracts from our connection?

Step 3: Identify and Strengthen Your "Fortress"

Create a visual representation of your "marriage fortress" on paper or in your journal. Draw a castle or fortress and label each wall with a boundary or principle you've agreed on as a couple (e.g., "No phones at dinner," "Weekly date night," "Pray together daily"). Add a "gatekeeper" label, symbolizing how you'll monitor and reinforce the boundaries together.

Step 4: Create a Support Plan

Choose one specific area where you feel your marriage is most vulnerable and take immediate action. For example:
- If past hurts linger, schedule a time to discuss and resolve them with honesty and forgiveness.
- If work hours are interfering, have a conversation with your boss about adjusting expectations.
- If technology is a distraction, set a rule for device-free quality time.

Document your chosen action and set a deadline to review your progress together.

INSIGHT

Use this area to write additional insights from the readings, reflection questions or activity responses.

CONCLUSION

As we come to the close of this journal, it's important to remember that marriage is not a destination, but a lifelong process of growth, love, and faithfulness. The sacred union between you, your husband, and Christ as the foundation requires continual care, attention, and spiritual nurturing. This book has explored what it means to build a Christ-centered marriage, rooted in God's design for love, covenant, and unity. But the real work begins now, as you live out these principles in the day-to-day reality.

You have learned the importance of roles and responsibilities, submission as mutual reverence to God, building intimacy in every area, and overcoming challenges with biblical wisdom. Each lesson is a tool for you to grow not only as a wife but as a woman of God who is committed to her calling, her husband, and the kingdom purpose you are building together. Marriage is meant to reflect Christ's love for the church—a love that is sacrificial, unwavering, and transformative.

Yet, marriage is not just about you and your spouse; it's about the legacy you create. It's about the example you set for future generations, showing what it looks like to honor God in your relationship. It's about guarding your heart and your marriage against the temptations and distractions of the world. Your love and commitment, when rooted in Christ, will stand as a testimony to the power of God's love, grace, and faithfulness.

The central question is: **"How do you differentiate between love as an emotion and love as a choice in your relationship?"** This is vital because there will be moments when you may not feel lovable or feel like loving your partner. During those times, it's important to remember that commitment isn't based on fleeting emotions but on a deliberate choice. Love as a choice means intentionally deciding, with God's guidance, to nurture yourself, your union, your family, and your foundation in Christ.

As you continue on this path, let this book be a foundation and a reminder of the sacred promise you've made. Remember, God is with you every step of the way, strengthening your bond, guiding your journey, and blessing your union. Together with your king from the King, you can build a marriage that not only stands the test of time but flourishes under God's grace. Keep Him at the center, and everything else will follow.

REFLECT

How has your relationship with Christ shaped the kind of spouse you desire to be? What characteristics do you want to reflect in your marriage that mirror Christ's love?

_____

_____

_____

_____

_____

_____

_____

_____

_____

_____

REFLECT

What steps can you take today to align your heart with God's will for your life and marriage? Which topic (e.g. challenges, intimacy) mentioned in this journal do you feel you will have the greatest challenge and how do you plan to prioritize and address it effectively?

_____

_____

_____

_____

_____

_____

_____

_____

_____

_____

_____

_____